I THINK THERE IS SOMETHING,
MORE IMPORTANT THAN BELIEVING:

ACTION!

THE WORLD IS FULL OF DREAMERS,
THERE AREN'T ENOUGH WHO WILL MOVE
AHEAD AND BEGIN TO TAKE CONCRETE
STEPS TO ACTUALIZE THEIR VISION.

~ W. Clement Stone, *businessman, author, and philanthropist who parlayed $100 into an insurance empire*

"This book is simply bursting and overflowing with powerful stories, quotes, resources and fresh ways to transform and grow in every dimension!"

~ SARK, *artist and author of "Creative Companion"*

THE POWER OF POSITIVE
DOING

BJ GALLAGHER

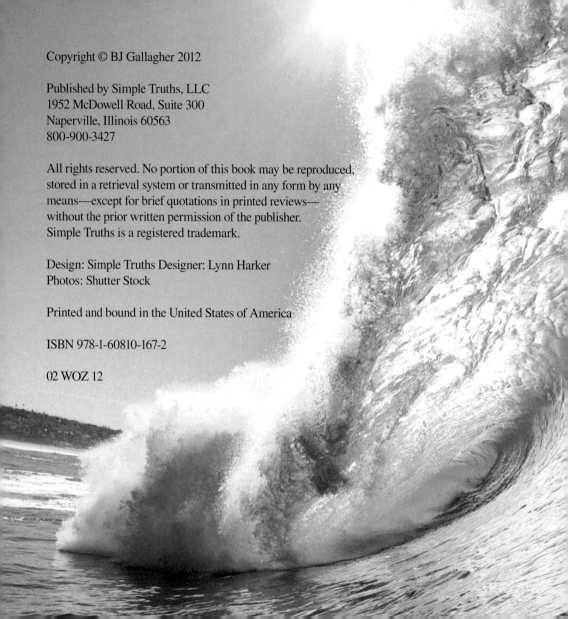

Published by Simple Truths, LLC
1952 McDowell Road, Suite 300
Naperville, Illinois 60563
800-900-3427

Design: Simple Truths Designer: Lynn Harker
Photos: Shutter Stock

Printed and bound in the United States of America

ISBN 978-1-60810-167-2

02 WOZ 12

"Life isn't about
finding yourself.
Life is about
creating yourself."

~ George Bernard Shaw, *Irish-born playwright*

The Power of Positive Doing
      MEANS TAKING **ACTION** ...

FOREWORD

One of the highlights of my life was my friendship with Norman Vincent Peale, author of *The Power of Positive Thinking*. After having been a fan of his for many years, I finally met him in the mid '80s and we became good friends. We even wrote a book together, *The Power of Ethical Management.* I really loved the man—he was a terrific human being.

One of the things he used to say was that, "a lot of people misunderstood the power of positive thinking … they thought that all you have to do is think positively and everything is going to work out." He said, "No, you have to also take some action, learn some skills—*you've got to do something."*

Here was one of his favorite stories about that:

> *"There was a guy that every day prayed to the Lord to win the lottery. He said, 'I'm a good Christian; I take care of my family; and all I want to do is win the lottery.' He prayed every day for six months, but he didn't win a cent. He got nothing.*

> *"He was angry and very disappointed. So he went to his prayers and said, 'Lord, I've been praying every day for six months. I'm a good Christian; I take care of my family. All I want to do is win the lottery, and I've got nothing.'*

"The sky got dark, thunder rolled, and a booming voice came out of the sky: 'Do me a favor, will you? Buy a ticket.'"

Norman loved that story and so do I. Yes, of course, positive thinking is important. But Norman Vincent Peale would point out that positive DOING is just as important.

As philosopher poet Henry David Thoreau said, "If you have built castles in the air, your work need not be lost; that is where they should be. Now put the foundations under them."

I'm thrilled that my friend BJ has written this book. I'm a raving fan of her work, and I'm sure that when you read this book, you will be, too!

Ken Blanchard,
Chief Spiritual Officer,
The Blanchard Companies,
and coauthor of *The One-Minute Manager*

The Power of Positive Thinking is all the rage these days. "The Secret" video and book, and others like it (Abraham-Hicks, Jack Canfield, Eckart Tolle, and Wayne Dyer's books and programs) are reaching millions of people who seek to live happier, healthier, richer lives. This is all wonderful. The human mind is an amazingly powerful computer, capable of transforming our lives—no doubt about it.

But achieving what you want in life isn't accomplished by sitting in your comfy chair and visualizing all day long. There's an action component to all this positive thinking. Far too many people neglect to ACT on their own behalf in order to bring their dreams to life. As cosmetics company founder and CEO Estee Lauder put it so well, "I didn't get here by dreaming about it or thinking about it—I got here by doing it."

In fact, I'll go one step further and let you in on a "secret" no one is talking about yet—**you can actually change your thoughts and attitudes by taking positive ACTION, no matter what you're thinking or feeling!** I call it "The Power of Positive DOING"—and that's what this book is about.

I've spent the past 20 years validating this idea in my own life, as well as the lives of the people with whom I work. I've used this approach as a mom—encouraging my son to take positive actions, even when he didn't feel like it. I've shared the idea with friends and professional colleagues—helping them see how we can act to make good things happen, shaping our thoughts and emotions in the process. This book is the culmination of two decades of practicing the Power of Positive DOING and helping others to do the same.

The book is divided into six chapters, each based on an Action Principle. Taken together, they spell:

ACT your way to right thinking.
CREATE new habits.
TAKE STEPS FORWARD, no matter how small.
INITIATE desired changes.
OPENLY WELCOME support from others.
NEVER GIVE UP on yourself.

My goal is to help you see that you are not the prisoners of your thoughts—you can take powerful, positive actions even when you don't feel like it. Read on. You'll see what I mean.

The Power of Positive Doing
MEANS TAKING **ACTION** ...

ACT your way to right thinking.

A
C
T
I
O
N

"If you want a quality,
   act as if you already have it."

~ William James, philosopher, psychologist

THOUGHTS LEAD TO ACTION ...
AND
ACTION LEADS TO THOUGHTS

Early in my career I attended a terrific seminar taught by Ken Blanchard, coauthor of the best-seller, *The One Minute Manager.* Ken said many useful and practical things in that workshop, many of which still guide me today. One of the best was: "It's true that people who feel good about themselves produce good results," Ken said. "But it's also true that people who produce good results feel good about themselves."

He went on to explain that no one knows how to change people's self-esteem, but we do know how to change their behavior. "So let's start with behavior," Ken continued, "and the self-esteem will follow." Ken was right on target and his teaching that day has helped me enormously.

For thousands of years, wise, insightful people have pointed out the power of our thoughts to shape our destiny. Simply put, we become what we think about. "If you want to change your circumstances, you must change your thinking," these smart men told us. They were right, of course. Our thoughts lead to words; our words lead to behaviors; our behaviors lead to habits; our habits form our character; and our character determines our destiny. And it all starts with thoughts.

The problem is, some of us have difficulty managing our thoughts. "My mind has a mind of its own," I often joke to my friends. Sometimes I can tame my mind and channel my thoughts into a positive direction. But other times my mind seems to run amok—thoughts and ideas race around in my consciousness like drunken monkeys, screeching for attention, chattering endlessly, determined to be heard and heeded. Changing my thinking in such moments is an impossible task—I don't know which monkey to grab first.

Then I remember what Ken said: It's hard to change internal things like negative thoughts, beliefs, attitudes and self-doubt. It's much easier to change external things, like behavior. So start by changing a person's behavior, and lo and behold, the attitude and beliefs will fall into place. You can literally help people to act their way to right thinking.

So on those occasions when my mind is unruly and resisting my attempts to tame my thinking, I ignore my thoughts alone and just get into action. I "act as if" I have a positive attitude, even when I don't feel it. Because when I "act as if," sooner or later my attitude always shifts.

As I get things done, that sense of accomplishment makes me happy, and my spirits lift. If I'm feeling insecure, anxious or self-doubting, the best thing I can do is start moving and do something—anything! Mow the lawn, wash the car, clean out a filing cabinet, help a friend, run some errands, file papers, organize my desk, do a load of laundry, walk the dog—getting stuff done makes me feel good about myself, even if I felt crummy when I started.

Ken Blanchard was right:

"People who feel good about themselves produce good results …

AND people who produce good results feel good about themselves."

We can literally act our way into right thinking.

"You have to pretend you're 100 percent sure.
You have to take action; you can't hesitate or hedge your bets.
Anything less will condemn your efforts to failure."

~ Andrew Grove, founder and CEO of Intel

TRUTH CONVERSATIONS

Fear comes in many forms. Some fears are rational and healthy—they keep us safe. Other fears are irrational—they keep us living small. The fear of what others might think of us, the fear of failing, the fear of looking foolish, or the fear of letting others down—all these can keep us from taking chances to pursue what we really want. Andrea Tobor has known such fears, up close and personal. I asked her to tell me her story.

"The year was 1992 and I was 41 years old, working for Time Warner in Chicago," Andrea began her story. "I was the director of a new division which was growing rapidly. We were having significant success—so much so that I was offered the job of vice president, at twice the salary I was making. A promotion is something that everyone looks forward to, and I did, too. But I was also scared to death. Moving up meant taking on a whole new level of responsibility. It meant leaving the safety and security of what I knew. It meant making a mental transition to move into a whole

new league and playing ball with the big boys."

"It sounds exciting, exhilarating," I said.

"Terrifying is the word I would use," Andrea replied. We both laughed.

"You see, in the corporate world, you have a public persona. You have this image that you've carefully cultivated and polished. The motto is 'Never let 'em see you sweat.' As a manager or executive, you're supposed to be cool, calm and collected—especially if you're a woman. No displays of feelings are allowed. So I looked together on the outside, but inside, I was in turmoil. I kept vacillating back and forth about this promotion I'd been offered. Should I? Shouldn't I?"

"Were you actually considering NOT taking the promotion?" I asked.

"Oh yes," Andrea answered. "I was scared to death. At that point in my life, I didn't know if I had what it takes to move up into executive ranks."

"So, how did you decide?"

"I turned to my inner circle of close friends and my family," Andrea replied. "I had two teen-age kids, a few trusted colleagues, and some dear friends. We had some major truth conversations."

"What's a truth conversation?"

"It's based on an ancient tradition of people sitting in a circle and telling the authentic truth to one another," Andrea answered. "In my case, the truth conversations with my friends and colleagues took place in small groups, and the truth conversations with my kids were done one at a time. I sometimes joke that my friends and family 'ganged up on me,' but it was really a very loving process. They simply weren't allowing me to escape the reality of who I was. It was almost like an 'intervention' of some sort."

"A career intervention?"

"Yes, that's a good term for it—a career intervention," Andrea responded. "My loving friends and family would challenge my fears, doubts and insecurities. They would tell me the truth about who I really was—as they saw me. They changed the conversation in my head. As my son summarized it, 'Mom, it's time for you to step into your own press releases.'"

"I love that. He said it perfectly!" I nodded.

"Yes, he did," Andrea agreed. "I am so blessed to have truth-tellers in my life—people who will remind me who I am when I forget."

"And you took the job?"

"Yes," Andrea replied. "I still had some fear, but I was able to take action in spite of my fear. I acknowledged my feelings but didn't let them control me. I took action.

"The career intervention worked. Those truth conversations allowed me to get to know myself and trust myself. And from that time on, I've never had self-doubt in the same way. Anytime fear comes up for me, I can go back in my mind to those truth sessions and tap into that loving courage again."

"If you were to give advice to others who are facing fear or other negative emotions, what would you tell them?"

"It sounds like such a cliché, but it's true ... Fake it til you make it,'" Andrea said. "I have a Georgia O'Keefe quote posted on the wall in my office. It's been there many years; I've referred to it innumerable times to guide my work and my life:

> 'I've been absolutely terrified every moment of my life—and I've never let it keep me from doing a single thing I wanted to do.'

"So ACT even if you don't fully embrace the thinking. Do not allow your fear to stop you from stepping into your life. That's the advice I'd give to others."

For more information about Andrea Tobor, visit her website: www.ecopresspartners.com

"We all have skepticism, fears and doubts. The difference between those who succeed and those who don't is that successful people learn not to let these feelings be an excuse for failing to take the necessary actions that will bring them success."

Steve Harrison, *founder of the Million Dollar Author Club and publisher of Radio-TV Interview Report (RTIR)*

"YOU CANNOT ALWAYS CONTROL YOUR THOUGHT BUT YOU CAN CONTROL YOUR WORD, AND EVENTUALLY THE WORD IMPRESSES THE SUBCONSCIOUS AND WINS OUT."

~ Florence Scovel Shinn, *author of The Power of the Spoken Word*

WHAT'S IN A WORD?

Assess your options.

Call up your courage.

Take your first steps.

> "YOUR FUTURE DEPENDS ON MANY THINGS,
> BUT MOSTLY YOURSELF."
>
> ~ Frank Tyger, philosopher

> "*Do you want to know who you are?*
> *Don't ask.*
> ***ACT!***
> *Action will delineate and define you.*"
>
> ~ Thomas Jefferson

THE *Princess* AND THE CRIMINAL*

by BJ Gallagher

Once upon a time in ancient China,
  there lived a beautiful princess.

One day, her father the king announced
that he would give his daughter's hand in marriage
   to the noblest,
     kindest,
       most honest man in the land.

Many men, eager to marry a beautiful royal wife,
  came to woo the princess.

One of these men was a criminal
   who had heard that the princess would be choosing
    from among her suitors.

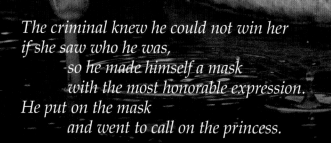

The criminal knew he could not win her
if she saw who he was,
     so he made himself a mask
       with the most honorable expression.
He put on the mask
       and went to call on the princess.

When she met him,
she was very taken with his impressive mask.
"I think I shall marry this one,"
      she told her father.
"For clearly, he is the noblest,
       kindest,
           most honest man
              among all the others."

The king announced a wedding date
      for one year hence.

The criminal was thrilled
      with his victory.

But at the same time he realized,
"I could lose her during the coming year,
    if she finds out who I really am."

So for twelve long months
he acted as if he were courageous and noble.
He acted kind and compassionate,
    attentive and loving,
        honest and honorable.

The princess grew to love him more and more,
    and he felt the same about her.

But when the morning of their wedding day
dawned,
    he became conscience-stricken.
He loved her so much,
    he could no longer deceive her.

He went to her and confessed.

Of course, the princess was hurt and angry.
"Take off your mask immediately!"
    she cried.
"Now I shall see who you really are!"

He did as he was commanded.
He removed his mask
        and stood before his beloved.

The princess gazed upon his face
        for the very first time.
"Why did you hide your face?" she asked.
        "It's identical to the mask!"

By choosing to act with noble character
        all year long,
                the criminal transformed himself.

The princess was so relieved and happy,
        she fell into his arms
                and they shared their first kiss.

                The couple married that day
                        and lived long happy lives –
                        TOGETHER.

* adapted from an ancient Chinese story

ACTION TIP:

~ *Practice Esteemable Acts* ~

When do you feel good about yourself? If you're like most people, you feel good when you accomplish something—reach a milestone or a goal—do something kind for someone else.

It can be as basic as washing your car or cleaning off your desk. It might be simple as letting someone else go first in line at the store, or helping someone who needs assistance. Such simple, daily acts can make you feel downright virtuous. And that's the point.

If you want to feel good about yourself, do something to trigger that feeling. Do something esteemable. Get something done. Take action on your to-do list. Help someone. Give to someone. Take care of something that needs your attention.

Make a list of acts that make you feel good about yourself. Then, whenever your attitude is a bit negative, or your mood is gloomy, or your self-esteem is in the basement—get out your list of esteemable acts and do something on that list.

People who do good things feel good about themselves.

START NOW.

The Power of Positive Doing
      MEANS TAKING ACTION ...

A

CREATE new habits.

T

I

O

N

"Action may not always bring happiness,
        but there is no happiness without action."

~ Benjamin Disraeli, British statesman and novelist,
England's first and only Jewish Prime Minister

THE HAPPINESS HABIT

"Most people are about as happy as they make up their minds to be," Abraham Lincoln once wrote. I've long thought so, too. Happiness seems to be a habit as much as anything—a habit of perception, a habit of attitude, a habit of responding to life, a habit of action.

I recall seeing a sign in a manager's office a number of years ago. It read:

"Happiness is available. Help yourself."

I loved the double meaning—"help yourself" as if a big bowl of happiness was sitting on his desk, like a bowl of jelly beans, and all you had to do was dip your hand in and help yourself—and "help yourself" as in "take action on your own behalf."

It reminded me of one of my all-time favorite books, *Happiness is a Choice*, by Barry Neil Kaufman. Barry and his wife had a baby boy, their third child, who was diagnosed as autistic. At first, the couple was devastated—they thought their lives were ruined and their child doomed to a hopeless future. But once they worked through their initial reaction to the diagnosis, they made a huge choice: They decided to be happy. They said, "We can let this situation drag us into depression and self-pity, OR we can decide to love our child, make a nurturing family for him, and have a good life together. They chose the latter.

They rejected the advice of doctors who told them to put the child in an institution and move on with their lives. Instead, they completely redesigned their home and their lives to meet the needs of their autistic toddler. He couldn't meet them in their world, so they met him in his. They sat on the floor and played with him, mimicking his shrieks, whoops and wild gestures. Bit by bit, they were able to build rapport with their son, teach him new behaviors, and coax him further and further into normalcy. The boy grew and thrived under his parents' unconditional love, patience, and teaching—it was a long, challenging process, but he graduated from high school, then college, with honors. And throughout those challenging years, Barry Neil Kaufman and his wife chose to be happy. They made it a habit.

How do you make happiness a habit? Simply choose it. Again and again. Habits are formed by repeating the same thing over and over again until it becomes the normal way you behave. Scientists tell us that if you repeat something consistently for 21 days, it will become a habit.

So, if you want to really feel the *Power of Positive Doing*, start by making happiness your new habit.

"HAPPINESS IS A STATE OF ACTIVITY."

~ Aristotle, *ancient Greek philosopher*

Joe Donlan has been many things in his life—an athlete, a businessman, a husband and father, a Marine, a good friend, and … a lifetime smoker.

"I smoked for forty years," Joe told me. "Back in my day, everybody smoked. We didn't have all the health information that's available today. We smoked; we drank; we ate fatty foods. Who knew?"

"So when did you quit, and why?" I asked.

"Well, let me backtrack a little," Joe responded. "In 1990, I went to a cocktail party one night and met a wonderful woman named Joan Hill. She had been a smoker on and off her whole life, too. So we started dating, fell in love, and began a very happy relationship—which we still have today.

"Joan was the director of public relations at the USC Marshall School of Business. In the early '90s, USC announced that it was going smoke-free. Joan thought about it for awhile and decided it was time to quit. She has quit at other times in her life, but this time she decided to quit for good. When she told me of her decision, she said, 'I'm going to quit smoking. You are welcome to continue smoking, if you

like, but just not in my condo.' I understood completely and I appreciated the respectful way she handled it.

"Shortly thereafter, a business colleague of mine had his 60th birthday party. After the party, I went with a former Marine buddy of mine to have a couple drinks at a bar on the way home. I stopped at a corner store to pick up a pack of cigs.

"When I woke up the next morning, I went downstairs and found what was left of the pack of cigs—there were only two left. It suddenly hit me. Between 4 p.m. on Friday night and 8 a.m. Saturday morning, I had smoked almost an entire pack! I thought to myself, Joan is going to quit smoking soon, so this is a good time for me to quit, too. I threw those last two cigarettes in the trash and I haven't smoked since. I just quit cold-turkey. That was May 6, 1993."

"Wow, that's amazing! Was it hard?"

"IF YOU DON'T DO WHAT'S BEST FOR YOUR BODY, YOU'RE THE ONE WHO COMES UP ON THE SHORT END."

~ Julius Erving, *basketball star*

"Oh yes," Joe replied. "The first three weeks, I was climbing the walls."

"Some time ago I read an article about a research project rating addictive substances on a scale of one to 100," I said. "These doctors ranked nicotine at 99. Heroin and crack cocaine were ranked 98 and 97 on this scale of addictiveness. I was shocked. I had no idea. I've never been a smoker myself, so I didn't know how powerful that stuff is. After that, I had new compassion for smokers. It must be so hard to withdraw from nicotine—not just the drug itself, but the habit—the lighting up, the ritual of smoking after meals, at cocktail parties. I can understand why it's so hard for smokers to quit."

"You're absolutely right," Joe responded. "It's a very tough habit to kick. That's why I never let myself have even one cigarette. Because I know that if I did, I'd be right back at the corner store buying a whole pack. The only solution for me is to never touch the stuff again."

"What advice would you give others who want to kick a bad habit, especially a health habit?" I asked.

"You have to take control of your life," Joe replied. "You have to really want to change, and then make the effort to change. You have to be positive. You have to make a decision. If you're not ready to change, that's OK. Just be honest with yourself. You can't give up something until you're really ready. It's your body and you can do what you choose. But in order to change something—whether it's smoking, drinking, exercise, eating, whatever—you have to WANT to!"

"Habit is habit and not to be flung out of the window by any man, but coaxed downstairs a step at a time."

~ Mark Twain, *humorist, satirist*

WHAT'S IN A WORD?

Honestly assess what's not working.
Adopt new behaviors.
Be consistent.
Intend to improve.
Take time to practice.

"MOTIVATION IS WHAT GETS YOU STARTED.
HABIT IS WHAT KEEPS YOU *GOING.*"

~ Jim Rohn, *motivational author and speaker*

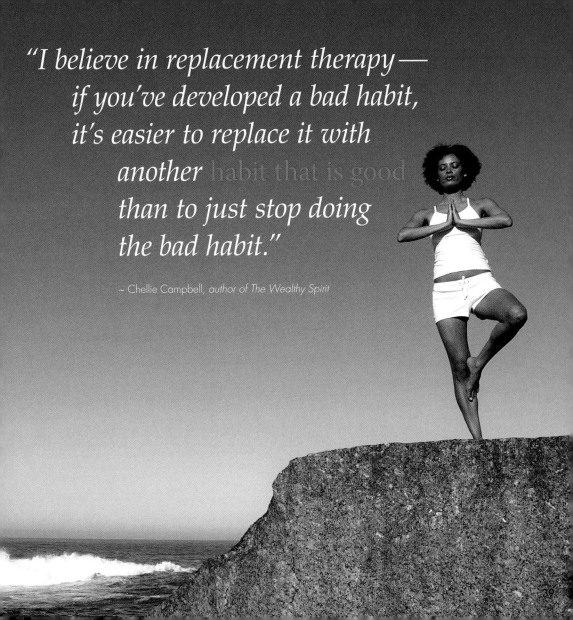

"I believe in replacement therapy—
if you've developed a bad habit,
it's easier to replace it with
another habit that is good
than to just stop doing
the bad habit."

~ Chellie Campbell, *author of The Wealthy Spirit*

HABITS

When I was a little girl
I had a bad habit—
I bit my fingernails down to the quick.
My mother told me to stop
but I couldn't …
        or wouldn't.

My mom scolded me,
        teased me,
                chided me—
                        she even cried.
But nothing did any good.
I still bit my nails.

The one day,
She decided to fine me 5¢
        for every time I bit my nails.

So I stopped.
I wanted my money
        more than I wanted to munch on my nails.

Some years later,
I had another bad habit.
I ate too many sweets and they made me fat.
My friends told me to stop
but I couldn't …
        or wouldn't.

I tried diets,
        and diet pills,
                and weight-loss programs.
But nothing did any good.
I was still fat.

Then one day,
I met a wonderful man
        and fell in love.

So I stopped eating sweets.
I wanted my sweetie
        more than I wanted the sweets.

And many years later,
I had another bad habit.
I drank too much all the time.
I told myself to stop,
but I couldn't …
        or wouldn't.

I tried switching to beer,
    drinking things I didn't really like,
        or limiting the number of glasses.
But nothing did any good.
I just bought bigger glasses.

Then one day,
I met some loving people
    who told me about a Higher Power.

So I stopped drinking.
I wanted **Spirit**
    more than I wanted spirits.

How did I change my bad habits?
By finding something I wanted more—
    by finding a higher good—
to help me trade in my bad habits
    for good ones.

It's SIMPLE, really ...
    but not always easy.

"We are what we repeatedly do.
Excellence, then, is not an act,
but a **habit**."

~ Aristotle, *ancient Greek philosopher, physician*

"EFFECTIVENESS, IN OTHER WORDS, IS A HABIT."

~ Peter Drucker, *professor, author of The Effective Executive*

ACTION TIP:

~ Learn How To Change Your Habits ~

You didn't develop your habits overnight — they evolved over many years. So don't expect to change them overnight, either. Be patient with yourself, and acknowledge yourself when you see the progress you're making.

It's best not try to take on all your habits at once. Pick one at a time, and spend several weeks or months working on it. Start with a small habit you'd like to change—set yourself up for success— then work your way up to tackling some of the bigger things you want to change about yourself.

In changing your attitude or a habit, you will go through four predictable stages:

The first stage is Unconscious Incompetence. This is when you are doing something that is not in your own best interest, but you are unconscious of the fact that you are doing it. You can't change at this point, because you don't even know that you need to change!

The second stage is Conscious Incompetence. This is when you wake up to the fact that you have a habit that is not desirable. Sometimes this is a rude awakening, when the light bulb goes on in your head, and you say, "Oh my gosh, look what I'm doing!" Sometimes this step is taken when someone else points out your problem behavior.

The third stage is Conscious Competence. This is when you adopt new behavior in place of the old, but it feels awkward and strange, because it is new. You are acutely conscious of feeling odd about your newly adopted behavior because it is not yet a habit.

The final stage to personal change is Unconscious Competence. This is when the new behavior has become habitual and you don't have to think about it anymore. Your new habit is now solid and you can relax in your new way of being.

The Power of Positive Doing
MEANS TAKING **ACTION** ...

A
C
TAKE STEPS FORWARD,
I
O no matter how small.
N

"Keep on going and the chances are you will stumble on something, perhaps when you were least expecting it. I have never heard of anyone stumbling on something while sitting down."

~ Charles Kettering, *inventor, founder of Delco*

MOST CHANGE IS EVOLUTIONARY, NOT REVOLUTIONARY

"Inch by inch, it's a cinch," my mother used to tell me, "but yard by yard, it's really hard." Mom was a wise woman, indeed. She isn't well educated but she is smart, insightful, practical, and she's taught me many important life skills.

It wasn't always easy to accept and learn what Mom tried to teach. I am not a very patient person, so my natural inclination is to do things in big chunks—or not at all. For instance, I like to write for hours or days at a time, when I'm inspired and turned on by an idea. I am not one of those methodical, disciplined writers who paces herself and writes for an hour or two every morning, day in and day out. I much prefer big bursts of creative energy, write a book as if I were running a marathon, and then, once finished, not write again for weeks, or months. This "inch by inch" stuff just ain't my natural style.

But my all-or-nothing approach to doing things did not serve me well when it came to many aspects of life. If I didn't have time to clean the whole house, I wouldn't clean any of it. If I didn't have enough time to start and complete a project, I just wouldn't start. And even with my writing, I discovered that if I wait until I have sufficient time to write an entire book, I would end up with not many books!

So I learned to "chunk" my writing—and other things as well. Time management experts teach this as a way to break a big project down into smaller, more manageable pieces. That way, if I don't have time to do everything, at least I have time to do *something*.

If I don't have time to clean the house, I'll clean one room. If I don't have time to organize my desk, I'll just tackle one pile of paper. If there's only an hour available, I might work on one book chapter, instead of the whole book. By breaking my projects into small chunks, I actually get more done than if I waited for big blocks of time to work on something.

This is a great approach to achieving goals. It's a terrific way to change a negative attitude into a positive one. It's a practical way to bring about change in your life. What small steps can you take—what chunk can you tackle right now—toward your goals and dreams?

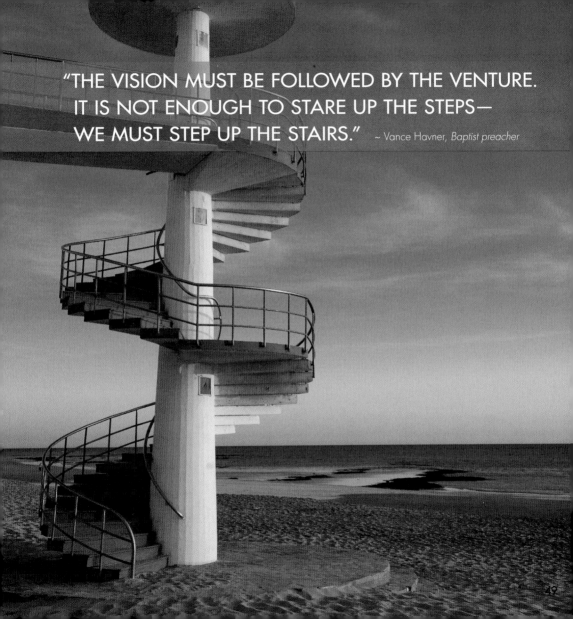

"THE VISION MUST BE FOLLOWED BY THE VENTURE.
IT IS NOT ENOUGH TO STARE UP THE STEPS—
WE MUST STEP UP THE STAIRS." ~ Vance Havner, *Baptist preacher*

Author, activist, and therapist Cathy Conheim is a woman who knows how to make things happen. "Wishing, waiting, and hoping—that's the language of victims," Cathy asserts. "Those are all passive words. They're not active. If you want things to happen in your life, you have to get moving—even if it's just one small step."

"Tell me more about that," I asked.

"A goal is not doable," Cathy replied. "A goal is a destination, an outcome, a result that you want. But you don't *do* a goal—you do actions that lead you to your goal.

"For instance, if you want a job, you write a resume. That's an action. Then you check job posting web sites—another action. You pick up the phone and make a call to follow up on a resume you sent—still one more action. You go on the interview—that's a big action. See what I mean? Accomplishing something—anything—requires you to start taking steps in the direction of your goal."

"Some people feel overwhelmed by a job search, or finding a mate, or looking for a great place to live," I said. "The goal looks so big, they don't know where to start. So some folks do nothing at all. They think, *It's hopeless*. What would you say to them?"

"Start with one small step," Cathy replied. "Just because you can't do everything doesn't mean you can't do *something*.

"Some years ago I took on a goal of raising $115,000 to buy a specially-equipped Freedom Van for Chris Timmin, a paraplegic woman here in San Diego. Chris had broken her neck in a terrible car accident; her husband left her; and her journey back from disaster had been hard and harrowing. When I met her, she had come so far in rebuilding her life—winning back her teaching job so she could be self-supporting, and so much more. But her 25-year-old van had finally given out and she

needed a replacement. The question was: How could a paraplegic school teacher ever buy a $100,000+ vehicle on her salary? She couldn't.

"So I committed to helping Chris. And you know what? Within nine weeks, we raised the money — all by e-mail, without using a single postage stamp! Here's how we did it: We sent out 50 e-mails to people we knew, people who trusted us. We explained the situation and told them, 'We promise you that every cent you send us will go to pay for the van. Not a penny will go to administration!' We also asked them to go one step further — 'Send this e-mail to ten people you know who trust you. Make the same promise to them that we made to you, and request that they pass along the request to ten more people who trust them.' This is important — we were building a community of trust. There are so many fund-raising scams out there — we needed for people to trust us and to trust one another.

"We kept our promise and they kept theirs. For the first two weeks, we received checks from people we knew. But by the third week, we were starting to get money from people whose names we didn't recognize. The network was working, and our community of trust was doing its job.

"What made this feat all the more remarkable is that it happened at a time when the San Diego area was ravaged by the worst wild fires in our history. It was a terrible time to try to be raising money. People were feeling helpless and hopeless in the face of such a community disaster. This is a common problem—people get so overwhelmed in the face of others' needs, that they often do nothing. They think, *What can I do? I'm just one person.* They don't think that one person can make a difference or that what they have to offer counts.

"Our story is bigger than just getting a Freedom Van for Chris—it's the story of showing people that they can make a difference, even if it's just sending in $1, or $5 or $10. We got a lot of small contributions in those months. We didn't need a big important wealthy donor—we just needed lots of individuals, regular folks, to give what they could. We are NOT paralyzed as people—there is always something we can do, no matter how big the problem. By taking action, any action, people can overcome their own personal sense of paralysis.

"People are glad to be part of something that makes a difference. If everybody picked just one other person to help, the world would be transformed. It's everyday people who are the real heroes—they just don't realize it.

"Small steps build momentum," Cathy continued. "Small actions build upon one another and pretty soon you're making good progress toward whatever it is you want. Whether you're doing a project to help others or pursuing a personal goal, the process is the same. Take that first small step forward, then another, and another. These steps generate energy and pretty soon the energy carries you forward with much less effort. You've started a process that takes on a life of its own."

"What advice would you give others?" I asked Cathy.

"EVEN IF YOU FALL ON YOUR FACE,
YOU'RE STILL MOVING FORWARD."

~ Victor Kiam, *businessman*

"It may not seem like much when you take that first step, but it is. For in that first step, you declare your intent, and the universe starts to align to support you in what you're up to.

"Second, I'd repeat what I said earlier: Just because you can't do everything doesn't mean you can't do something.

"Third, I'd point out that you have three resources at your disposal: time, money, and energy. If you don't have any money right now, dedicate time and energy to your goal. If you have money but no time, then write a check and pay someone to act on your behalf. You can always be doing something to forward the action toward what you want.

"And finally, I'd say 'keep your eyes and ears open.' Sometimes you start out with one idea in mind, but the goal can change as you take action. Stay flexible; be open to new opportunities. Sometimes a totally new goal can evolve out of your actions—something more magnificent than you could have ever imagined. But you'll never find out what the universe has in store for you if you don't take that first step.

Cathy Conheim has a new passion and a new project, writing books to raise awareness and raise money for animal rescue groups, disadvantaged children, and kids in military families whose parent(s) are fighting overseas. To find out more, visit her web site www.henrysworld.org

WHAT'S IN A WORD?

See new possibilities.
Test limits.
Engage all your senses.
Prepare for success.
Set sail toward your future.

"There are no mistakes. The events we bring upon ourselves, no matter how unpleasant, are necessary in order to learn what we need to learn. Whatever steps we take, they're necessary to reach the places we've chosen to go."

~ Richard Bach, *author of "Jonathan Livingston Seagull"*

The goal of many dog owners is to be as wonderful as their dogs think they are. Annie Brody's story is one of love, companionship, personal challenges and heroism. She was every bit as good a best friend to him as he was to her.

"Someone once told me that you should name your dog for the characteristics you want him to have," Annie Brody said, "So I named my dog Hero. I thought it was a good idea, in case I ever got into a jam and needed a hero."

Little did she know how right she was.

Annie had always loved dogs, ever since she was a little girl. But she grew up in a housing complex in Manhattan where pets were not allowed. "Dogs always brought me joy," Annie said, "and I was always drawn to them my whole life.

"When I went to college at Cornell, I wanted to study to be a veterinarian, but my science grades weren't good enough. So I ended up getting a degree in communication instead. Then when I started my career, my job took me on the road a lot, so it never seemed to be a good time to have a dog.

"But then they started opening dog parks in Manhattan. I recall one day I was coming home from work and saw one of my neighbors in the hallway. He had a golden puppy named Kona. I bent down to pet the dog, engage with her on her level, and make friends with her. Afterward, I went into my apartment and suddenly realized that my entire energy field had changed. I felt excited, happy, relaxed, and sort of glowing—like I'd just met a new friend that I liked a lot. I thought, *Oh my god, I got that from the dog!*"

"Sounds like a revelation, an epiphany," I commented.

"It was," Annie nodded. "I said, 'I'm not going to put this off anymore.' And within two weeks I adopted Hero from the local ASPCA. He was a golden retriever, about one or two years old."

"So tell me what it was like — did your life change when you adopted Hero?"

"What I recall most is how I began to see the world through his eyes," Annie said. "I noticed how noisy the city was, how much grey, sharp-edged concrete there was, and the lack of green living things. There were people pushing, always in a hurry. It was intense and anxiety-making. Over time, I began to not like the city anymore. I wanted to live in a place where Hero and I could feel more peaceful, enjoy lots of greenery, and where he could run free off leash.

"So I moved to Columbia County in the upper Hudson Valley. It's real rural and farm-like here. I loved it and so did Hero. In fact, we loved it so much that I got inspired to start a new venture—it's called Camp Unleashed (where city dogs and their people go to "ruff" it.). Twice a year, people come here with their dogs and we spend a long weekend together in the countryside and the woods. The dogs have a great time and their human companions get to learn more about them and experience them as their true doggie selves—playing together in a pack, free of the leash and in nature. The dogs are great teachers. It's an amazing experience."

"Yes, they are great teachers," I nodded. "I feel that way about my dog, too."

"One day Hero and I were out walking and he stumbled badly. It turned out he broke his femur. I rushed him to the vet, who did X-rays to assess the damage. She discovered a large tumor—osteosarcoma—and told me the prognosis was not good. Standard treatment is amputation, followed by chemotherapy and/or holistic treatment. But life expectancy would only be a few months. Hero was nine years old and I was determined to give him every chance at a long life. I told the vet I would do whatever it took to save him.

"The amputation was performed the next morning. I'll never forget watching Hero as he came out of the anesthesia and tried to get up and take his first steps. At first he was a little confused, like, *What's wrong here?* Then he took a couple halting steps, trying to get his balance. I could practically see his brain trying to make sense of this new situation.

"And suddenly he got this look on his face, like, *Oh, I get it.* And within just a couple more minutes, he was moving around just fine. I swear, the whole process of learning to walk again took him only five minutes! I was so impressed and inspired by him.

"He was an amazing dog. There was no whimpering or whining. He didn't spend any time feeling sorry for himself or complaining. He just adapted to his new reality and got on with the business of living."

"Hero lived happily for another three years after that. He was a therapy dog, a Delta Pet Partner, and he visited kids with cerebral palsy. Hero was such a gentle, patient dog. I'm sure those kids felt the same glow that I felt when I first met my neighbor's dog years earlier."

"You certainly named him well, didn't you?"

"Yes," Annie said softly. "Hero died when he was twelve, but he's still my hero today. He taught me so much about life and love. He taught me about adaptability—about dealing with life on life's terms. He showed me that there is no value in self-pity or lamenting 'why me?' His resiliency was remarkable—magnified by his courage and grace.

> "A NON-DOER IS VERY OFTEN A CRITIC — THAT IS, SOMEONE WHO SITS BACK AND WATCHES DOERS, AND THEN WAXES PHILOSOPHICALLY ABOUT HOW THE DOERS ARE DOING. IT'S EASY TO BE A CRITIC, BUT BEING A DOER REQUIRES EFFORT, RISK, AND CHANGE."
>
> ~ Wayne Dyer, author of *The Power of Intention*

"Just last year, I thought of Hero when I got laid off from my job because of the bad economy. At first I was upset—that lasted about 24 hours. Then I remembered Hero and the way he had handled his own personal disaster. So after my initial shock from the layoff wore off, I told myself, I've been an entrepreneur before—I can do it again. I very quickly saw that this career setback could really be a blessing. I now had more time to build Camp Unleashed into a successful business. Before I always had to squeeze it in around my 'real job,' but now I could focus on what I really loved to do—get to know and play with lots of dogs and their people. Now, I could take Camp Unleashed to the next level.

"I immediately got into action: I started visioning what I wanted the business to look like; I reached out to others and let all my friends and colleagues know what I was up to; I contacted the Small Business Development Office and enrolled in a program with them. I got a mentor and wrote a business plan. I realized I could professionalize what I loved.

"So next year I plan to double the number of camp sessions we have. We just finished our first winter camp and it was amazing. I want to expand to other locations. Like Hero, I'm adapting. There's no self-pity here. Like I've always said about Hero: He lost his leg but not his heart."

"I just love your story, Annie. Thank you for sharing it with me. I have one last question: Do you have any advice for others?"

"Any advice I'd give would be what I learned from Hero," Annie replied. "When bad things happen, it's OK to be shocked, hurt, and/or confused—just don't get stuck there. Process your feelings as quickly as you can and move on. You can't go back and change what happened to you, so just accept it.

"Second, don't take it personally when something bad happens. Nobody's picking on you; God isn't punishing you; you're not a victim of Fate. Life just happens—good stuff and bad stuff—everybody gets some of both.

"And finally, keep looking forward. No matter how bad yesterday was, today is a new day, and tomorrow is another. Hero loved to ride in the car with his head out the window, feeling the rush of air on his face, taking in all the sights, sounds, and smells coming at him. I don't recall him ever looking backward—he was always looking forward to see what was coming next, or to the side to see what was happening around him. That's a good way to go through life."

For more information about Camp Unleashed, contact Annie Brody at www.campunleashed.com

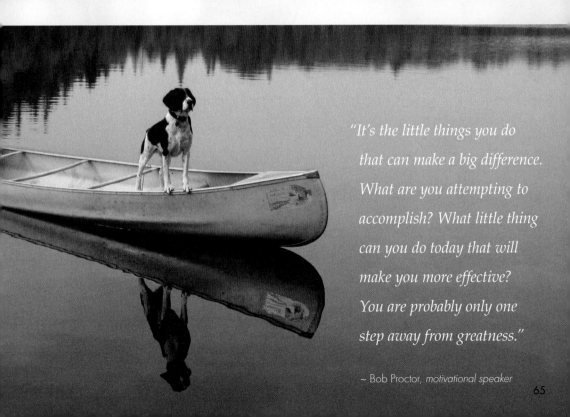

"It's the little things you do that can make a big difference. What are you attempting to accomplish? What little thing can you do today that will make you more effective? You are probably only one step away from greatness."

~ Bob Proctor, *motivational speaker*

STEPS

by BJ Gallagher

I wish my life had a straight trajectory,
success piled upon success,
ever higher.

But alas,
It isn't so.

It's two steps forward,
one step back.
My progress is quite uneven.

Sometimes, one foot gets stuck,
and I find myself going in circles.

I have to get my foot unstuck
before I can straighten out
and more forward again.

Once in awhile I misstep,
   and stumble
     or fall.

When this happens,
   I sometimes cry.
"I was doing so well
and suddenly I took a tumble.
The going can be so hard sometimes."

Then I wipe away my tears,
   get to my feet again,
     and take the next tentative step.

Other times,
   I laugh when I fall.
"Oh, silly me,"
   I chuckle.
"I should've paid more attention.
Anybody could have seen this coming."

I enjoy a good laugh,
   and get moving again.
"That was a painful lesson
   I won't soon forget."

Occasionally,
my progress seems like
   two steps forward,
   three steps back.

"Well, that's not good,"
   I mutter to myself.
And I try to figure out
   where I went wrong.

But in the long run,
  what really matters is:

Did I take more steps forward than backward?
Did I have some great experiences along the way?
Did I take a few exciting detours?
Did I help my fellow travelers along the way?
And, did I give thanks for every step of the journey?

If "YES,"
  then my life is a ***success.***

ACTION TIP:

What Three Simple Things Can You Do Today, To Move You Closer To Your Goals?

First, think about your bedroom. Now, list three simple things you could change about your bedroom that would make you happy. Nothing complicated—nothing expensive—just three simple things you could easily change. (ie, rearrange your furniture; put different sheets on the bed; move the TV out of your bedroom; put a colored light bulb in the lamp to create a different mood; etc.) List these three simple changes on a piece of paper—*now go do them!*

Next, think about your car. List three simple things you could change about your car that would make you happy. *(ie, new seat covers; clean out the trunk; put some different CDs in the car to listen to; etc.)* Write these three things down—***now go do them!***

Next, think about where you work —your office or cubicle or workspace. Now, list three simple things you could change about your workspace that would have you happy. Nothing complicated, nothing expensive—just three simple things that are within your power to change. (ie, get a new cushion for your chair; put a new screensaver on your computer; rearrange your office furniture; etc)
Now get busy and make these three changes!

You can do this easy exercise for any aspect of your life—your health habits, your resume, your family life, your leisure time, your finances, or even your spiritual life. You'd be surprised how small changes can shift your attitude and mood very quickly.

You'll also be amazed at how quickly these small changes add up to bigger changes! **START NOW.**

The Power of Positive Doing
MEANS TAKING **ACTION** ...

A
C
T **I**NITIATE desired changes in your life.
I
O
N

"They say that time changes things,
but you actually have to change them yourself."

~ Andy Warhol, *multi-media pop artist*

ACTION
ALLEVIATES ANXIETY

For many years, I suffered from tension headaches with painful symptoms: impaired vision, sensitivity to light, excruciating throbbing in my temples, and sometimes nausea. They were awful. I consulted with doctors and dentists; I tried various medications; I took up meditation and tried bio-feedback. Some things helped a little bit—but nothing seemed very effective for any length of time.

Then I discovered something interesting—that taking action eased my headaches. Physical action was the best—anything that got my body moving. I could mow the lawn, wash the kitchen floor, workout in the gym, do some laundry, work in the garden, wash windows, wax the car—anything physical. Getting my body into action enabled me to work out the tension that was causing the headaches.

Other types of action worked, too—calling a trusted friend and having a good conversation; having sex (though that isn't always an option); writing in my journal; going for a long, relaxing drive. In short, any action that I can take to dissipate the pent-up tension in my head will do the trick. My head feels better; my neck and shoulders relax; and I feel the satisfaction of having done something.

Perhaps your anxiety doesn't show up in headaches. Maybe you carry your tension in some other part of your body—your back, your stomach, your shoulders, your intestines, your sinuses. Doctors estimate that as many as 80 percent of the physical problems their patients report are stress-induced!

Taking action to discharge the pent-up energy caused by stress can prevent health problems, and can even cure some of the ones you might already have.

Getting started is half the battle. A body at rest tends to stay at rest and overcoming our own inertia is a huge step forward. If you can get yourself to take just one step forward, you're now in motion—and a body in motion tends to stay in motion.

When my car won't start, I call on AAA. When my happiness won't start, I call on the other Triple A—Action Alleviates Anxiety. So can you!

"TUNE OUT THE NAYSAYERS,
TUNE INTO YOUR OWN COURAGE,
AND TAKE A BOLD STEP TOWARD THE
PASSION-FILLED LIFE YOU REALLY WANT."

~ Oprah Winfrey, *talk show host, actress, media entrepreneur*

Debbe Kennedy is living the life of her dreams — with a lovely home on the California coast, a thriving consulting business, and a rich, fulfilling personal life. Such wasn't always the case for Debbe — she spent many years climbing the ladder in one of the world's most prestigious corporations. I asked her to tell me how she initiated such a big change in her life:

"I suppose it started with a *stirring* inside me. At first, I was more startled by the feeling than frightened, because I had intentionally set the time for the wake-up call some twenty years earlier during my very first week working at IBM.

"I was twenty-two years old and living a dream-come-true

in my new job in a beautiful high-rise in Los Angeles. One of those first mornings, I was standing by my desk, when a beautiful woman executive walked in. Her office was a short distance away. She was very tall with a kind regal presence that commanded attention ... and I gave it to her. I had not ever seen an 'older' woman like her before. She was graceful; dressed in the most elegant, understated way; in black with a long strand of pearls and very expensive looking shoes.

"As I stared at her while she unlocked her door, a colleague came walking by, whispering to me with a deliberate cadence that let the words slowly slide out one by one, 'Do - you - know - how - long - she's - worked - for - IBM?' She asked; then answered, 'Thirty - four - years.' It sounded like a horrifying *life sentence* to me at twenty-two. I couldn't even imagine it. So, I vowed that very minute that I would never allow someone to whisper about me in that way. I would know when it was time for me to leave and do it gracefully."

"And did you?" I asked.

"Well, as most of us discover, time flies," Debbe replied. "The years seemed to have been in a constant fast-forward with a corresponding, ever-increasing stack of milestones and miracles. I loved IBM. My career flourished. My work was satisfying and empowering. It wasn't perfect—but by all standards, it was a grand, value-based place to work."

"Ah, I sense there's a *'great place to work, BUT…'* coming up in this story," I said as I leaned in.

"Yes, you're right," Debbe continued. "Fast forward twenty years: What started initially as a stirring inside me, soon turned into a series of quite powerful jolts—small earthquakes shaking my grip on the status quo. All kinds of unexpected signs kept showing up. The experience left me terrified—paralyzed by what it meant—unsure of what it would ask of me. I felt confused about the strange feelings inside, while I couldn't point to anything being wrong, I had a blazing fear of leaving IBM.

"Then came the turning point that mobilized my first bold move. We were in the process of transforming the company and training leaders company-wide. Our leadership team was trained in guided imag-

ery—at IBM, we called it 'thinking.' During the training, we drew pictures of our personal vision. I remember vividly the moment I claimed my wings. 'I want you all to know that I am leaving,' I announced, holding up my drawing with great pride, 'I'm not sure exactly when, perhaps in five to nine years, but I am leaving and you should be happy for me.' Even now, trumpets sound as I trace my freeing words and remember the shock on my team members' faces."

"And then … ?"

"Some weeks (not years) later, IBM announced a window of opportunity to leave. You had to be within twelve years of retiring totaling thirty years service or you forfeited lifetime health care. I was three years short. But I left anyway.

"Thinking is easy, acting is difficult, and putting one's thoughts into action is the most difficult thing in the world." ~ Johann Wolfgang von Goethe, *German poet*

"At my exit interview, the IBM executive asked me if I was sure I wanted to leave, knowing I would not have my lifetime medical coverage. From somewhere inside my answer came, 'What if I could earn enough to pay for my own health care? Wouldn't that be a better vision?'"

"So you spread your wings and flew the coop. What did you do next?"

"I took flight in 1990 and started a business with my best friend Sally. We put the uncommon pairing of leadership and graphic art together to form what is today Leadership Solutions Companies. We are now celebrating two decades of success, for which we are deeply grateful. The health care benefit plans changed shortly after I left. I would have lost a year of freedom, if I had stayed. I remain forever indebted to IBM for all I learned there that made my dream come true.

"I would describe my life's metamorphosis with the wise words of Emmet Fox:

'... so the wonderful thing happens: the butterfly emerges beautiful, graceful, now endowed with wings, and instead of crawling about on a restricted leaf, he soars above the trees, above the forest itself — free, unrestricted, his own True Self.'"

For more about Debbe's work, visit www.puttingourdifferencestowork.com

"*Until you dream, there isn't a mold.*
Until you speak, there isn't a promise.
And until you move, there isn't a path."

~ Mike Dooley, *author of Manifesting Change*

The Power of Positive Doing

ACT your way to positive thinking.

BOUNCE back and begin again.

CONTRIBUTE to others' success.

DELIGHT in every bit of progress.

EXPECT positive results.

FIND purpose and meaning in life.

GO where the love is.

HONOR your values by living them.

INSPIRE others with your positive example.

JUMP into new adventures.

KEEP your commitments.

LEARN to dance with change.

MAKE friends worth having.

From *A* to *Z* ...

NURTURE body, mind and spirit.

OVERCOME obstacles and roadblocks.

PARTNER with kindred spirits.

QUESTION self-limiting beliefs.

REACH OUT for help when you need it.

STEWARD your money well.

TAKE ON a new project.

USE your head and your heart.

VEER away from complainers.

WATCH for unexpected opportunities.

XPRESS your creativity.

YAWN in the face of fear.

ZERO in on what's truly important.

WHAT'S IN A WORD?

Create your own future.
Hanker for something new.
Alter your course.
Navigate uncharted terrain.
Go your own way.
Embrace the unknown.

"A PESSIMIST SEES DIFFICULTY IN EVERY OPPORTUNITY.
AN OPTIMIST SEES OPPORTUNITY IN EVERY DIFFICULTY."

~ Sir Winston Churchill, *British Prime Minister*

"We must be willing to let go of the life we have planned so as to have the life that is waiting for us."

~ E.M. Forster, *English novelist*

CHANGE

by BJ Gallagher

I've heard it said that
  "People don't like change."

But that's really only half-true.

People make changes all the time:

We change clothes,
  change restaurants,
    change cars,
      and change our opinions
      about all sorts of things.

We change schools,
  change jobs,
    change careers,
      and change our minds
      about what's important to us.

We change houses,
  change spouses,
    change friends,
      and change direction
      whenever we want to.

The real truth is
    we LIKE changes
        we choose for ourselves.

*And the changes we **don't** like*
    are the changes
        imposed on us by others.

Because really
it's the feeling of powerlessness,
    and not being in control,
        that we don't like.

There is something deep in the human spirit
    that resists being told what to do.

We have within us
    an instinct for self-determination.

So we must choose our own changes
    as much as we can,
lest we abdicate our lives to others.

"To exist is to change, to change is to mature,
to mature is to go on creating oneself endlessly."

~ Henri Bergson, *French philosopher, winner of the Nobel Prize in Literature*

"Your time is limited, so don't waste it living someone else's life. Don't be trapped by dogma—which is living with the results of other people's thinking. Don't let the noise of others' opinions drown out your own inner voice. And most important, have the courage to follow your heart and intuition. They somehow already know what you truly want to become. Everything else is secondary."

~ Steve Jobs, *founder and CEO, Apple*

ACTION TIP:

~ *Focus On What You Can Do,* *Not What You Can't Do.* ~

The human mind is a "mis-match detector." It always notices what's wrong before it notices what's right. For instance, if you walk into a room that has ten paintings on the walls, with nine of them level and one of them crooked, what will you notice first? The crooked painting, right? Of course. And it's not just you—everyone's mind is like that. We immediately notice what's wrong in any situation.

This isn't a problem except when it comes to trying to make a change in our lives. Then, this "mis-match detector" doesn't serve us very well. We think of all the things holding us back; we imagine all the ways our plans could go awry; we project all the problems with an idea before we even try to make it work. Our minds tend to focus on what we can't do, rather than what we can.

This doesn't mean you're a negative person—it just means you've got a normal mind that has a negative default position. All you have to do is recognize this fact, and then retrain your mind. It takes a bit of time and practice, but it's very doable.

Simply focus your attention on what you can do. Team up with a friend and brainstorm, if you like. Make a list of the possible actions you can take. Focus on things you can control—not things over which you have no control.

If you find yourself drifting back into "I can't" thinking, simply redirect your thoughts. So, "OK, I see what I can't do, now let's spend some time looking for what I can do."

Training your mind is not unlike training a puppy. With consistency, gentle discipline, redirection of attention, and regular reinforcement, you can retrain your mind to focus on the positive. **TRY IT.**

The Power of Positive Doing
MEANS TAKING ACTION ...

A
C
T
I
OPEN UP and ask for help and support
N

"'Please help me' are three of the most
powerful words in the English language."
~ Cathy Conheim, *therapist and author*

NO ONE CAN DO IT FOR YOU, BUT YOU CAN'T DO IT ALONE

Self-reliance is a laudable strength, but it can also be a serious weakness. Failure to seek support from others in achieving your goals can mean the difference between exhilarating success OR frustration, isolation, and exhaustion from trying to go it alone.

In American society, we tend to over-value the individual and under-value community. We wholeheartedly subscribe to the myth of the rugged individual—John Wayne, the Lone Ranger—the strong silent type. And we often fail to appreciate that fact that there is ample research and evidence to prove that we all do better when we team up with others.

Do you know how much weight a Clydesdale horse can pull? This magnificent, one-ton animal (best-known as the horse breed that pulls the Budweiser beer wagon) can pull 5,000 pounds by himself. What if you team up two Clydesdales? Do you think their pulling capacity doubles? If so, you'd be wrong. The pulling power of a pair of Clydesdales is several times the pulling capacity of one horse!

The synergy between the two horses increases their work capacity exponentially.

And so it is with people, too. Together we are greater than the sum of our parts. Two heads really are better than one, especially if the two heads are smart enough to know that they're more creative and productive together.

We humans are designed to live and work in relationship with one another. So, as you're developing the Power of Positive Doing in your own life, remember to reach out and ask for help. Let others support you. Learn from them. Lean on them when you need to. You are still responsible for your own life and your own success, but don't think you have to do it all by yourself.

"IN HELPING OTHERS, WE SHALL HELP OURSELVES,
FOR WHATEVER GOOD WE GIVE OUT COMPLETES
THE CIRCLE AND COMES BACK TO US."

~ Flora Edwards, *South African-born industrialist*

95

WEALTH AND WELL-BEING

Sam Beasley is a millionaire. Twenty-five years ago he was homeless and hopeless. How did he take his life from one extreme to the other? I asked him to tell me his story.

"You're a successful businessman today—you own commercial real estate and several businesses," I began. "I can't imagine you ever being on the skids. How did you ever end up being homeless? What happened?"

"I got divorced, I lost my business, and I got depressed," Sam replied. "I just spiraled downward. I turned to alcohol and drugs to ease my pain, but they just made my depression worse. It finally got to the point that I couldn't take care of myself. Depressed people often find even basic self-care impossible and that's where I was—down for the count. I crashed on friends' sofas until I finally wore out my welcome and didn't have anywhere else to go. I started sleeping in garages, since I didn't want to sleep outside. That was my lowest point."

"What did you do?"

"I reached out for help and found a support group," Sam responded. "I got better advice from them than from anyone else in my life. They helped me pull up my self-esteem. They told me to get a job, which I did. They told me to buy groceries and eat healthy, so I did. I just did what they told me to do because clearly, my best thinking had gotten me nowhere.

"I didn't realize at the time how depressed I was. Losing my marriage was bad enough, but to lose my business on top of that was just too much. Business setbacks are particularly difficult for men because we get so much of our identity and self-respect from work and making money. I look back now and I can see that I was depressed. And of course, the booze and drugs just made it worse.

"I vowed I would never go back there again. Through the help of my support group, I was able to get stable. The job I got came with a truck, so I had wheels again. I was able to become self-supporting and do the basics in terms of taking care of myself. I returned to college. Eventually I married. I finished school and got a better job doing work I loved.

"But then I discovered credit. I knew nothing about credit cards and really didn't understand how they worked. I'm a smart guy, but I'd never had any exposure or experience to teach me about the responsible use of credit cards.

"I was still rebuilding my life and so I started to use credit to speed the process along. I got in over my head. It got to the point that I couldn't cover my expenses. In short, I had put myself at risk *again.* Thank God, this time I didn't have to go so low."

"What did you do to get out of hock?"

"This time I knew to ask for help sooner," Sam replied. "I asked people in my support group for their advice. 'How do you not incur debt?' I asked them. It sounds kind of silly, I guess, telling the story now. But really, I didn't have a clue how to live life without using credit.

"Then I began to ask other people—folks outside my support group. I watched for people who looked like they had money and set out to learn from them. I was willing to ask for advice. It was awkward in the beginning, but I discovered that most people love to be asked—they're happy to help.

"Most important, I was willing to do what these people said. I trusted them. I wanted what they had, so I was willing to do what they did."

"What did these people tell you?"

"One of the first things they told me was 'every time you get paid, save a little and give a little.' So I did it. I would take a little of each paycheck and sock it away, and take a little and give it to charity or someone else who needed help."

"What else?"

"I used to have breakfast all the time at the same coffee shop," Sam continued.

"I noticed a group of men who were there every time I was and I began to watch them. They all looked successful—they wore nice clothes; they drove nice cars; they seemed confident and self-assured. So then I began to sit with them. I didn't talk much—I just listened to them. And I began to copy them."

"What else did you learn from these guys?"

"I found out that they were all in real estate," Sam said. "They each had their own real estate brokerage. I learned that the vast majority of millionaires in America made their millions through owning their own businesses. So I made a note of that.

"I noticed that all of them knew what things cost. So I began tracking my

spending and writing down how much everything cost that I bought. I did it without understanding it or knowing what would happen. I was willing to mimic others without understanding why they did what they did. It was a blanket decision: *If I do what they do, I will get what they got.*

"I began to ask more questions of these men I was having breakfast with every day. At the time, I thought I might write a book about what I was learning, so I approached it like that. And I started to ask for referrals: 'Do you know any other successful guys I could talk to?'

"What did they teach you?"

"I discovered that at one point in their lives, they all had nothing," Sam answered. "That was a surprise. I would never have thought that, just looking at them. So that gave me hope. They had come from nothing and were now millionaires, so I figured that I could do it, too.

"They taught me several things:

1. **Get a mentor.** None of these guys knew how to be successful—they had learned it from others.

2. **Pray ... a lot.** Some of the men I interviewed met with others every morning for prayer. Some had a mastermind group. Prayer was an important part of their daily routine.

3. **Give to others**. Without exception, all these guys talked about giving. One guy said he wished he had learned about giving much earlier in his career. He told me, 'You can't out-give God.' He'd never lost by giving to others.

"My best thinking had led me to homelessness, hopelessness and despair. These magnanimous men, and my support group, taught me to put aside my own thinking and act on faith instead. I often had no idea why I was taking action, except I trusted the good people around me. I see now that I was acting my way to right thinking."

"What did you do with all that learning?"

"I decided that I couldn't just write a book. I had to do all the things they had taught me. I thought it would be disrespectful not to use it. So that's what I've done. And today, I'm where they're at. In fact, I might be doing better than some of them," Sam chuckled.

"I finally understand what it was that I saw in those men—it was the peace that comes with prosperity. It was the absence of fear, the absence of stress. Those men exuded extraordinary peace, extraordinary relaxation."

"What advice do you have for others who want to act their way to right thinking?"

"It starts with the basics," Sam replied. "Take care of yourself. Eat healthy, wear clean clothes, surround yourself with friends worth having, find or build a supportive community, go back to school if you need to.

"I got more and more inspired by what I was learning and by the supportive community I had found. Eventually, I wrote a book with my wife, Suzanne, titled *Wealth and Well-being*. The book's message is: Self-Care leads to Self-Worth, which leads to Net Worth.

"In our country, we have a cultural belief that the money comes first—then it leads you to self-worth, which leads you to good self-care. It's actually just the opposite, and my life is a good example. I had to start with self-care because I had no self-worth and certainly no net worth.

"It's not easy to take care of yourself if your self-esteem is in the basement.

But if you do it anyway, no matter how you feel about yourself, you'll find that self-care will build your feeling of self-worth. And the more you take care of yourself, the better you'll feel. You'll begin to have an experience of wealth in many areas of life—friendships, family, work, and health. Then the attaining and maintaining of net worth follows from that.

"Many people look at a rich person and say, 'Well, of course you can go to the gym and eat organic food and have a personal trainer—because you're rich.' But the truth is, self-care starts wherever you are. If you don't have a lot of money, you go for a walk instead of the gym; you exercise to a DVD in front of your TV instead of with a personal trainer; you buy salad stuff instead of burgers and fries. Good self-care doesn't require wealth—*it leads to wealth.*"

For more information on Wealth and Well-being, visit Sam and his wife, Suzanne, at www.wealth-wellbeing.com

TO MAKE DOUGH, **DO**."

~ Bertram Troy, *financial advisor*

"*Every morning I get up and look through the Forbes list of the richest people in America. If I'm not there, I go to work.*"

~ Robert Orben, *magician, author, comedy writer*

"IF YOU WANT TO LEAVE FOOTPRINTS
    IN THE SANDS OF TIME, WEAR WORK BOOTS."

~ anonymous

WHAT'S IN A WORD?

Hearing what's needed.

Eager to contribute.

Listening with compassion.

Paying attention to the little things.

Intuitively understanding what's helpful and what's not.

Never overstepping your bounds.

Going out of your way for a true friend.

Healing love, healing touch.

Asking "What can I do to help?"

Never assuming that you know what's best.

Desiring to serve and contribute to others' well-being.

Friends

by BJ Gallagher

What would I do without you?
You're always there for me,
in good times and in bad.

Cheering me on
when I'm discouraged;
Offering suggestions
when I get lost;
Nudging me gently
when I feel lazy;
Extending your hand
when I need some help;
Lending an ear
while I whine and complain;
Sharing your shoulder
when I just want to cry;
Giving me a big "thumbs up"
when I make good progress.

Words seem inadequate
to express my love and gratitude—
so I hope you can hear
the whispers of my heart ...

"Thanks, friend."

"MY FRIENDS HAVE MADE THE STORY OF MY LIFE. IN A THOUSAND WAYS, THEY'VE TURNED MY LIMITATIONS INTO BEAUTIFUL PRIVILEGES."

~ Helen Keller, deaf/blind author, activist, and lecturer

"*Each friend represents a world in us, a world possibly not born until they arrive, and it is only by this meeting that a new world is born.*"

~ Anais Nin, *French diarist*

ACTION TIP:

Who Are Your Champions? Your Fans And Supporters? Your Mentors And Coaches?

For many years I maintained what I called my "Golden Rolodex." It was filled with the names, phone numbers, and contact information of coworkers and colleagues, friends and family, and business contacts. It was "Golden" because it was so valuable to me. These people were my safety net, my support group, my mentors and coaches, people whose advice and encouragement I depended on to help me become successful and happy.

Today, nobody has a Rolodex anymore—they've been replaced by Blackberrys, smart phones, and other high-tech equivalents. But they're still Golden. In the event of a fire, flood, or earthquake, I venture to say that your personal digital device is one of the first things you'd grab as you headed for safety. And rightly so. Those people in your PDA are worth their weight in gold!

You undoubtedly have different people you go to for different kinds of support. If you need financial advice, you call financially savvy friends, or perhaps a professional money manager. If you're trying to change a personal habit, you call someone who has experience in dealing with a similar problem, or join a support group. If family matters are giving you fits, you call a trusted friend or confidante whose counsel you respect. In short, you've got a whole team of people who are ready, willing, and able to support you in the Power of Positive Doing.

Have you thanked them lately? Do you tell them how much they mean to you? Do you appreciate them in ways they recognize? Have you hugged your fan club lately?

But…what if you don't have a Golden Rolodex or Golden PDA full of champions, supporters, mentors and coaches? Then take action immediately. Make a list of the people you want to build relationships with. Successful people know that they need others. If you want to be successful, figure out who you want on your team and start investing in "the interpersonal bank" with them. You can't make withdrawals of time, attention, and energy if you've never made any deposits. It's never too late to start building your winning team! **GO GOLDEN!**

The Power of Positive Doing
     MEANS TAKING **ACTION** ...

A
C
T
I
O
NEVER GIVE UP on yourself.

"All things are possible until they are proved impossible—
and even the impossible may only be so, as of now."

~ Pearl S. Buck, *author, philanthropist*

"IMPOSSIBLE" MEANS,
"I'M POSSIBLE"

Years ago I was writing a book on autobiography and in my research discovered that the life stories that are really interesting and engaging are the ones in which individuals had to overcome obstacles and rise to meet difficult challenges.

Problems test our character and our ability. Obstacles challenge us to think creatively and figure out how to go under, over, around, or through them on our way to our goals. When the odds are stacked against us, we often rise to the occasion and surprise people ... including ourselves!

Many of us learn more from our struggles than we do from our successes. Hard times can be valuable teachers. Failure is often the precursor to success—showing us what we need to learn and where to put our energy if we are to achieve our dreams.

To be sure, struggle, disappointment and setbacks are not fun. A friend once told me that "experience is what you get when you don't get what you want." But invariably that experience proves to be a valuable resource.

Living life to the fullest means that when you take action, sometimes you fall on your face. And sometimes you give it all you've got—and still come up short.

But ultimately, what matters most is that you don't give up on yourself. Never. Ever.

"I have missed more than nine thousand shots in my career.
I have lost almost three hundred games.

On twenty-six occasions I have been entrusted to take the game-winning shot—and I missed.

And I have failed over and over and over again in my life.

And that is precisely why I succeed."

~ Michael Jordan, *basketball star*

NEVER GIVE UP

IT'S NEVER TOO LATE TO BE
WHAT YOU MIGHT HAVE BEEN

Ruth Lavigne was thirty years old when she started working with a therapist. She had just given birth to her second child and was experiencing some depression. She felt trapped in an unhappy marriage and unfulfilled in her work. She was a banquet waitress, working for her in-laws.

"I have a masters degree in international business," Ruth said. "Prior to moving to San Diego, my husband and I lived in Houston, where I had worked in a money management company. But I hated it. When we came to California I knew I didn't want to go back to an office job, so I started working as a banquet waitress. It may not have been challenging work—nor did it pay well—but it gave me flexibility so I could take care of my kids. I loved the change of pace from what I'd been doing in Houston. So I waited tables for several years.

"It was fine for awhile. And therapy helped a lot, too. It enabled me to sort out the sources of my depression and explore alternatives that might make me happier. I recall one day telling my therapist, Cathy Conheim, 'I want to tell my kids that they can be anything they want to be when they grow up, but how can I do that with any credibility?' I could just imagine my kids saying, 'And you wanted to be a waitress when you grew up?' I knew that I had to practice what I preached."

"What did you want to be when you grew up?"

"I had always wanted to be a doctor," Ruth replied. "But when I told Cathy, it sounded so stupid. I was too old to go to medical school; I had two kids to take care of; and my husband did drywall in construction—he certainly couldn't support our family if I went back to school.

PERSEVERE

"So I decided to be a medical assistant. At least that would put me in the field of medicine. I called my dad to ask if he would help me go to school. He's a doctor."

"And did he agree to help?"

"No," Ruth shook her head. "He said, 'I won't help you do that. If you're going to go back to school, do something worthwhile.'"

"It wasn't the answer I expected," Ruth said. "So I decided to go to nursing school instead. I went to classes early in the mornings, spent the afternoons with my kids, and waited tables at night.

"I recall telling my therapist, 'I love this. Being in medicine is so wonderful. But I'm so sad that I can't be a doctor.' She said, 'Yes, it's too bad that you can't be a doctor.' She was smart—she didn't disagree with me or try to tell me what to do. Instead, she met me where I was emotionally, and gradually helped me move forward so that I could see for myself how mistaken I was.

"Finally one day I asked myself, 'Why *can't* I be a doctor?' And she replied, 'I don't know. Why can't you? The only difference between you and the other doctors is that at the end of your life you'll have practiced medicine ten years less than they have.' She was so right. It was a HUGE breakthrough. I didn't want to be a nurse—I wanted to be a doctor."

"What did you do then?"

"I called my dad and he said, 'I'll help.' My mother-in-law offered to help by babysitting the kids. It was if the stars all aligned to support me once I'd made up my mind what I wanted to do.

"I spent the next four years taking pre-requisite classes to get ready for med school. I continued to work nights as a waitress and went to school in the daytime, finishing my post-baccalaureate pre-med program and earning straight As all the way. I applied to medical schools all over the place, but got accepted to just a few, including the University of Cincinnati—where they make room for non-traditional students like me. And at age 36—with two kids, five and six—I moved to Ohio and started medical school."

"And your husband went with you, too?"

"Yes, we all moved to Cincinnati to start a new chapter," she answered.

"It sounds like once you made your declaration of intent, the universe lined up to support you."

"Well, not the entire universe," Ruth chuckled. "You'd be surprised how many people told me I'd never make it. One parent said, 'You're gonna be 40 when you're a resident—you'll never make it.' And one of the guys at the gym said, 'You'll never get into medical school.' There were dozens of people who told me I was crazy, that I should give up my dream.

"But once you make the leap—once you say it out loud—you're committed. Medical school was hard. And when I got to my internship, it got really hard –the hardest thing I've ever done. It was a 13-year journey to become a doctor. But I couldn't give up on myself—I just couldn't. And finally, at age 45, I became a physician. Now I am a 49-year-old oncologist, specializing in breast cancer and pediatric cancer. I'm still at the University of Cincinnati and my kids are 18 and 19.

"Sometimes I feel a little sad about the sacrifices I made to pursue my dream—especially in terms of time I missed with my children. But I knew I needed to do something so I could take care of my family, since my husband doesn't work much or earn much when he does work. I used to fear that I would lose touch with my kids because I was working so hard in med school, but that didn't happen. We are closer than ever. And Cincinnati is a great place for kids to grow up—they've had a wonderful childhood here."

"Well, Ruth, you've come a long way from banquet waitress, haven't you?"

"Yes, it's been an incredible journey … from waiting tables to 'Best Doctors in America.'"

"You were voted one of the 'Best Doctors in America?'"

"Yes, every year for the past three years. And I was voted one of the 'Top Docs in Cincinnati' for 2009-2012, too."

"Wow! That's fabulous! Your story is a perfect illustration of what can happen when you don't give up. What advice would you give others, Ruth?"

"I'd tell people that it's attitude—not aptitude—that's most important. I am not the most brilliant person in the world. But it's all in motivation and determination. If you're committed to something, achieving a career goal, fulfilling a lifelong dream, then that's what counts the most.

"When people ask me how I got through all those difficult or unpleasant times, I say that I just did what had to be done. I didn't think about it too much. I was just committed to my goal. It's sort of like that old story about the centipede … if you ask a centipede how he walks, he gets so focused on his hundred feet that he forgets how to do it. I think that's what I did. I didn't get hung up on the 'how' of what I was doing — I just did it."

"The thing that is really hard, and really amazing, is giving up on being perfect and beginning the work of becoming yourself."

~ Anna Quindlen, *Pulitzer Prize-winning journalist*

"ACHIEVEMENT SEEMS TO BE CONNECTED WITH ACTION.
SUCCESSFUL MEN AND WOMEN KEEP MOVING.
THEY MAKE MISTAKES, BUT THEY DON'T QUIT."

~ Conrad Hilton, *founder of Hilton Hotels*

127

WHAT'S IN A WORD?

Persist no matter what.

Endure discomfort.

Request help from other people.

Steadfastly hold onto your beliefs and values.

Envision triumph.

Very consistently keep at it.

Embrace adversity as your teacher.

Refuse to give up.

Enjoy and celebrate every tiny bit of progress!

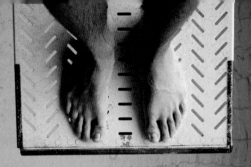

"... THERE IS SOMETHING YOU MUST ALWAYS REMEMBER:

YOU ARE BRAVER THAN YOU BELIEVE,

STRONGER THAN YOU SEEM,

AND SMARTER THAN YOU THINK ..."

~ Christopher Robin to Pooh

(A.A. Milne, author of Winnie the Pooh)

Without faith, nothing is possible. With faith, nothing is impossible.

~ Mary McLeod Bethune, *educator, civil rights leader*

by BJ Gallagher

There are days,
*   I must admit,*
when I just want to pull the covers over my head
and stay in bed.
Life can be hard
and I feel overwhelmed,
*   discouraged,*
*   and tired.*

"What's the point?"
*   I ask.*
"Why go on?
It's just too much to bear."

And sometimes I want to chuck it all,
*   move to a cabin in the woods—*
away from all the stress and striving,
*   my life would be simple and serene.*

Or, maybe I'll just run away
*   and join the circus,*
*   like I dreamed as a kid.*

Shall I be an acrobat?
*   A lion tamer?*
*   A fire eater or sword swallower?*
*   Maybe just a goofy clown.*

But then I wake up
    from my escape fantasies.
I realize that my life may be hard sometimes,
    but it's still MY life—
        it's all I've got.

And I'm worth something …

I'm worth getting out of bed for.
I'm worth giving life another shot.
I'm worth the effort,
    the struggle,
        and the pain.

Each day,
    each hour,
        each moment
is a new beginning,
    a new promise,
        a new possibility.

If I'm not for me,
    who will be?

It's never too late
    to be what I might have been.

ACTION TIP:

~ *"Just Say No"… To Hopelessness* ~

I'm a recovering perfectionist.

"What's wrong with being a perfectionist?" you might ask. "Aren't high standards a good thing?"

Well, yes and no.

Perfectionism makes you strive for excellence in everything you do—but it also has a tendency to make you judge yourself harshly when you don't live up to those lofty standards you hold. Most perfectionists are their own worst critics.

When a perfectionist makes a mistake, it's a very short step from, "I made a mistake" to "I AM a mistake."

When a perfectionist gets discouraged, it's a very short step from "It's hopeless" to "I'M hopeless."

Perfectionists may look like they have high self-esteem, but actually, their perfectionism is a mask to hide their true feelings of insecurity and self-doubt. Hopelessness is the fear that haunts most perfectionists.

So if Hopelessness has ever haunted you—dragging you into resignation and despair—remember the *Power of Positive Doing*, and **TAKE ACTION.**

- Make a list of all the things you're proud of in your life—attributes, accomplishments, obstacles overcome, tough times survived, and more.

- Call three friends and ask them what they most like or admire about you.

- Dust off your resume and send it out to a couple other employers — even if you don't want a new job. Knowing that you have career options will instantly make you feel better about yourself.

- Go do something you're really good at—to shrink your fearful Hopelessness back into proper proportion.

Say "NO" to Hopelessness … and say **"YES" TO HAPPINESS!**

THE POWER OF POSITIVE DOING CREED©

by BJ Gallagher

I believe that positive thinking must be accompanied by positive doing,
   and I commit to getting into action.

I believe that action alleviates anxiety,
   and I commit to taking the first step.

I believe that even when we can't do everything, we can always do **something,**
   and I commit to doing whatever I can, wherever and whenever I can.

I believe that little steps can bring about big changes,
   and I commit to putting one foot in front of the other.

I believe that we each create our own future,
   and I commit to being accountable for my choices.

I believe in focusing on what I **can** do, instead of what I **can't** do,
   and I commit to looking for possibilities and opportunities.

I believe that time is my most precious asset,
and I commit to making the most of each moment, each hour, every day.

I believe that success is about progress, not perfection,
and I commit to celebrating my accomplishments, no matter how small

I believe that life is lived in relationships with others,
and I commit to getting good at getting along.

I believe that there is no "I" in TEAM … but there is in WIN,
and I commit to making the winning difference.

I believe that true happiness and fulfillment come from serving others,
and I commit to living my life in service and contribution.

I believe that one person can make a big difference,
and I commit to being that person.

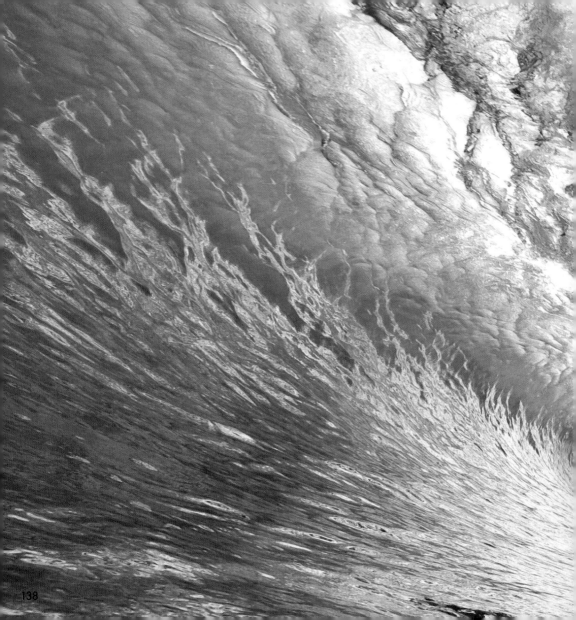

He could see a wave rising.
For once he was right.

The wave's coming; it's high,
its strong, and it's going to smack
him in the face...

Unless he **takes action** and
rides the wave.

Lynn Harker, *artist and designer*

ABOUT THE AUTHOR,
BJ GALLAGHER

BJ Gallagher is an inspirational author and speaker. She writes business books that educate and empower, women's books that enlighten and entertain, and gift books that inspire and inform. Whether her audience is corporate executives, working women, or spiritual seekers, her message is powerful, positive and practical— consistently focusing on the "power of positive doing."

She has written over twenty-five books, including an international best-seller, *A Peacock in the Land of Penguins*, now published in 23 languages worldwide. Her Simple Truths books include:

- *Learning to Dance in the Rain: The Power of Gratitude*

- *Friends ... the Family You Choose for Yourself*

- *The Road to Happiness: Simple Secrets to a Happy Life*

- *Oil for Your Lamp: Women Taking Care of Themselves*

BJ makes frequent presentations at conferences and professional gatherings in the United States, Europe and Latin America. Her lively presentations inspire and instruct audiences of all types—with a style that is upbeat, fast-paced, funny, dynamic and charismatic. Her clients include: IBM, Chevron, John Deere Credit, Chrysler, Raytheon, U.S. Department of Veterans Affairs, Volkswagen, the American Press Institute, U.S. Department of Interior, University of Illinois, among others.

BJ is frequently sought out as an expert on human relations and has appeared on the Today Show, the CBS Evening News, CNN, Fox News, and PBS. She gives hundreds of radio interviews on a wide variety of social problems and popular culture issues.

To contact BJ, visit her web site:
www.bjgallagher.com

What OTHERS are saying...

We purchased a Simple Truths' gift book for our conference in Lisbon, Spain. We also personalized it with a note on the first page about valuing innovation. I've never had such positive feedback on any gift we've given. People just keep talking about how much they valued the book and how perfectly it tied back to our conference message.

— **Michael R. Marcey,** Efficient Capital Management, LLC.

The small inspirational books by Simple Truths are amazing magic! They spark my spirit and energize my soul.

— **Jeff Hughes,** United Airlines

Mr. Anderson, ever since a friend of mine sent me the 212° movie online, I have become a raving fan of Simple Truths. I love and appreciate the positive messages your products convey and I have found many ways to use them. Thank you for your vision.

— **Patrick Shaughnessy,** AVI Communications, Inc.

simple truths®
Motivational & Inspirational Gifts

SMALL BOOKS THAT SPEAK VOLUMES

Be sure to enjoy our complete collection of e-books. You'll discover it's a great way to inspire friends and family, or to thank your best customers and employees.

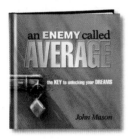

For more information, please visit us at:

www.simpletruths.com

Or call us toll free... **800-900-3427**

THE END

NO! *It's just the beginning.*